Broken and Blessed

How God Used One Imperfect Family to Change the World

A Preview Book

Jessica LaGrone

Abingdon Press
Nashville

BROKEN AND BLESSED:
HOW GOD USED ONE IMPERFECT FAMILY TO CHANGE THE WORLD:
A PREVIEW BOOK
Copyright © 2014 by Abingdon Press

All rights reserved.

No part of this work may be reproduced or transmitted in any form or by any means, electronic or mechanical, including photocopying and recording, or by any information storage or retrieval system, except as may be expressly permitted by the 1976 Copyright Act or in writing from the publisher. Requests for permission should be addressed in writing to Permissions Office, 201 Eighth Avenue, South, P.O. Box 801, Nashville, Tennessee 37202-0801, faxed to 615-749-6128, or emailed to permissions@abingdonpress.com.

This book is printed on acid-free paper.

ISBN 978-1-4267-7840-7

All Scripture quotations are taken from the Holy Bible, New International Version®, NIV®. Copyright © 1973, 1978, 1984, 2011 by Biblica, Inc.™ Used by permission of Zondervan. All rights reserved worldwide. www.zondervan.com. The "NIV" and "New International Version" are trademarks registered in the United States Patent and Trademark Office by Biblica, Inc.™

Library of Congress Cataloging-in-Publication Data on file

14 15 16 17 18 19 20 21 22 23 — 10 9 8 7 6 5 4 3 2 1

MANUFACTURED IN THE UNITED STATES OF AMERICA

Contents

Introduction 5

1. Adam and Eve 7

2. Abraham and Sarah 16

3. Isaac and Rebekah 25

4. Jacob and Esau 32

5. Rachel and Leah 44

6. Joseph and His Brothers................... 54

Notes....................................... 64

Introduction

Does your family have issues? Mine does, too. The good news is there's no such thing as a perfect family. Perhaps that's why I like Genesis so much; it tells the story of a perfectly imperfect family not too different from my own imperfect family, recording both the good and bad pictures of their experiences through the generations.

In this little book we will trace the Genesis family from Adam and Eve to Joseph and his brothers, introducing their stories and a few of the lessons we can learn from them (stories and lessons I explore in depth in my Bible study by the same title, *Broken and Blessed*).

Despite their brokenness, God chose to love and bless this family so that they might be a blessing. As we get to know each generation, noting both good and bad traits that were passed down, we will see that God worked for good in their lives for the good of the world. And we will see that God wants to do the same in our own imperfect families today, bringing blessing from brokenness.

Whether you're single, married, or divorced—with or without children or grandchildren—you have an important part to play as a member of God's family. Join me as we discover how God can transform and use us to bring blessing in a hurting and broken world.

1

Adam and Eve

Genesis 1-3

When you read the first sentence of Genesis, it's as if you were discovering the roots of your story for the very first time: "In the beginning…." Our hearts long to discover our beginnings. As Genesis opens, there is no question that this is the story of a loving Creator and His creation.

First a Home, Then a Family

The first chapter of Genesis is dedicated to God building a home for us: our world. This important chapter is written in a pattern spelled out as intricately as the creation it describes. Days 1–3 are a picture of the home, the environment God created. Days 4–6 are a description of the family,

Broken and Blessed

the inhabitants who will live there. Though Genesis 1 and 2 are different in many ways—each with its own distinct account of creation—both highlight humanity as the pinnacle, the masterpiece of God's already remarkable work.

The word for ground in Hebrew is *adamah*,[1] and the word for human—which encompasses both male and female—is *adam*.[2] That's where the first person gets his name, Adam, which means "human." That kind of word play, from *adamah* to *adam*, lets us know that God is doing something special to give humans a significant connection with their environment, the earth. We will soon see that when humans flourish, their environment benefits. When humans sin, their environment suffers along with them.

Into this dusty creature, as common as the ground we walk on, God breathes the breath of life. Suddenly we are infused with God's own breath. Of all the holy places on earth that God would choose to live, He chose to dwell inside His people—inside you and me.

With all the creatures surrounding him, the human is alone because there isn't another one like him. Even the presence of God Himself doesn't quite fit the need for this specific kind of

Adam and Eve

companionship that the adam longs for. Genesis 2 refers twice to the need for a "suitable helper" (vv. 18, 20). So God creates woman from man. The story of creation is complete only when this last step of companionship is in place. Humanity is now living in the companionship of family.

The Story of Sin

The next chapter, Genesis 3, is essential because it's the story of not only the first sin but also every sin. It describes Eve's temptation, but it's our story too. Eve and Adam's encounter with the serpent traces our human condition from head to toe. Every sin since has followed in their footsteps. Every relationship has been marred by the same consequences of blame and shame. And it all began so innocently, with a simple question: "Did God really say…?" (Genesis 3:1). The serpent's words are, of course, a misquote. Even God's words can be twisted. All temptation is a subtle attack on the character of God.

After twisting God's words, the serpent's next tactic is an out and out lie contradicting God: "'You will not certainly die,' the serpent said to the woman. 'For God knows that when you eat from it your eyes will be opened, and you will be like God, knowing good and evil'" (Genesis 3:4-5). The insinuation here is that God is holding something back from His children and cannot be trusted to have our best interests at heart.

Eve chooses to play God, taking matters of what's best for her and her family into her own hands and onto her own lips—and then onto her husband's. And the world is forever changed.

All we have seen so far is a God who interacts with perfect children in a perfect world. We may wonder: How will He react when things go wrong? And what will God do when this imperfect world is filled with imperfect humans? This is the question for all of us to consider, since we all live outside of Eden and we all sin—we all face the moment of coming before Him broken, asking for another chance.

Adam and Eve stand before Him, vulnerable, exposed, naked, and ashamed. Will He be wrathful? Angry? Cold? Rejecting? The moment of suspense is answered by the unexpected. Instead of wrath they are shown kindness. Instead of rejection, grace. Out of compassion God cares for them by clothing their nakedness, taking the scratchy, disposable fig leaves they've patched together and providing the first clothing the world has ever known—a wardrobe of grace.

The Consequences of Sin

When the woman tasted the forbidden fruit and offered it to her husband, who did the same, it didn't take long for those relationships to sting with the consequences of their actions. Ashamed, they hid from God, who called out for them.

Adam pointed the finger at his wife and then right at God: "The woman you put here with me." Eve responded with a classic: "The devil made me do it." Though they played the blame game, each of them admitted to eating the fruit. What follows in Genesis 3 is a list of the effects of sin that we are still dealing with today. The consequences are handed out in the order of action—first the serpent tempted, then the woman acted, then the man followed.

God's first commentary on how sin will spread into human lives has to do with the perfect relationship humans have had with their environment. Originally it was an environment so

Broken and Blessed

ecologically ideal that no one had to plant or water or weed. No one had to kill in order to eat. It was the best of all harmonized worlds—all play and no work. Now there will be struggle to produce, time spent in sweat and toil. Now identity will be bound up in the question "So what do you do?" and humans will confuse their worth with productivity, earning, rank, and success. The prediction that the eating of the fruit will result in death becomes clearer here as well. In Genesis 3:19 God says that they will return to the earth from which they came.

Human relationships with God and their earthly home will be different in this broken, post-sin world. God also explains how their relationships with each other will be affected. The woman is told that she will suffer consequences in an act that she has not yet even experienced: bearing children. God says, "I will make your pains in childbearing very severe; with painful labor you will give birth to children" (Genesis 3:16a). If this doesn't make you a little upset with Eve, it should! This means that we have Eve to thank for labor pains, swelling, and bloating; for episiotomies and hemorrhoids; for baby weight and postpartum depression. None of this was part of God's original plan in paradise. (Yet

Adam and Eve

because we probably would have done the same thing in her situation, perhaps we should offer Eve some grace. God certainly did.)

If we naively believe that the pain of childbearing is limited to labor and delivery, then we'll be surprised by our panic in a child's first trip to the emergency room and by the ache of watching them get on the school bus for the first time. Along with the joy of watching our children grow will come late nights of waiting up for them to come home, followed by sleepless nights wondering if they'll ever leave the nest. Show me a person, big or small, taking a step toward independence and behind him or her you will almost always find a mother watching with a bittersweet mix of pride and heartache.

Every parent knows the heartbreak of watching a child's heart break. Every parent would gladly take on a child's pain. Children are born in a moment, but they are borne through life with ongoing pushing, teaching, listening, loving, and grace. That's the lifelong nature of childbearing. Parents endure it because the result—the chance to love a human being who, like themselves, is made in God's image—is undeniably worth it.

The other relationship that begins to show consequences from sin is the one the woman shares with her companion, Adam. This has been the first model of human relationship, the gift of perfect human partnership created by God. Woman and man enjoy each other as perfectly matched companions. Now there exists a new gulf between them. Genesis 3:16 tells us that woman's desire will be for her husband and he will rule over her.

The kind of desire described here is not a loving desire or even a sexual desire. This is the beginning of a desire to control. Followed by the other half of the sentence, "he will rule over you," it means that both partners will struggle to exploit their relationship for their own gain, to control the other instead of enjoying the intimate bond and the life of mutuality they began in God's perfect creation. God's first blessing to His children, "Be fruitful and multiply. Fill the earth and subdue it," is now forever tainted with the pollution of human corruption.

Both the multiplying of relationships and the subduing of the earth just got a lot more difficult. Men will labor. Women will labor. Their relationships with God, their environment, and each other will have difficulties, brokenness. Life is going to involve hard work from here on out.

Adam and Eve

Strangely enough, there is a glimmer of good news in this list of consequences, which is embedded in God's message for the serpent. Genesis 3:15 says, "And I will put enmity between you and the woman, and between your offspring and hers; he will crush your head, and you will strike his heel." This "he," God says, will be one of Eve's offspring. He will receive an injury from the serpent, but in turn, He will strike the decisive blow in the battle. And He will eventually crush the serpent once and for all.

Inserted into the litany of consequences from the first sin we find a consequence the serpent probably didn't expect: God will fight for His children. God, who is always good and always ready to offer grace and second chances, had a plan to turn their brokenness into blessing.

*God's grace spreads farther than
the reach of any sin.*

There is no place outside the reach of God's love.

2

Abraham and Sarah

Genesis 12, 15, 16, 22

Between Adam and Eve and Abraham and Sarah, the human race deteriorates to a state of moral and relational bankruptcy. Even after God floods the earth and begins again, it doesn't take long for sin to spread and take over. Genesis is up front with us, providing a clear picture of what happens to humanity when we are left to our own devices. From Genesis 3 to 11, humanity brushes off God's guidance and walks its own path.

God must come up with a secret weapon so big and so powerful that it can repair the damage that has been done and somehow stop the recurring cycle of degeneration that repeatedly leaves the world in such a mess. What will this secret weapon be? What will God use to change the world?

Abraham and Sarah

God's Secret Weapon: A Family

Genesis 12 reveals that God's secret weapon is a family. That's all—one man and one woman with their future in God's hands. God offers Abraham and Sarah an opportunity to reshape human history. His plan is to bless their family so that through them all the people on Earth will be blessed.

God calls Abraham and Sarah to walk away from a clan that not only is passing down the practice of being self-protective and self-interested but also is likely polytheistic, worshiping false gods and idols. In the same breath God promises them something momentous and also asks something incredibly challenging of them. They are to leave behind the script that their families have handed them and many of the ways their families have formed them and look to God to teach them a whole new way of living. As they leave their families behind, He promises them that this new relationship with Him, this new life separate from the way they have been raised, will be one of tremendous blessing—but it comes with a reminder. You are blessed for a reason. Through you, my blessings will flow to the entire world. God's work in their lives and in the generations of their family is not for their sake only but also to create vessels worthy of being called His chosen people—set apart for a purpose, blessed to be a blessing.

When God wants to change the world, He starts with a family. It was true then. It's true now. God re-forms our families so that we can be conduits of His blessings.

God of the Desert

God chose to use a flawed family, one with imperfections, shining His glory through their cracks to bring light to the world. Abraham and Sarah's imperfect family includes struggle with inner character weaknesses, difficulties in their relationship, and one major physical obstacle to God's plan: they are childless. Since God has promised that an entire nation would be born through them to bless the world, this presents an immediate and serious barrier. It's a problem for Abraham and Sarah, who are far beyond childbearing years, and it's a problem for us, since we would really like God's presence in our life to be accompanied by an easy road, clear of any obstacles. But it's not a problem for God. God has no trouble working in difficult circumstances. In fact, He seems to enjoy it, using the toughest cases to work out His story in the world.

Abraham and Sarah's challenge is going to require learning a deep trust in a trustworthy God. Such trust is clearly not there yet for Sarah because when God's plan doesn't unfold as quickly as she expects, Sarah decides to make things happen herself. Sarah's solution involves sending her maid, Hagar, into her husband's bed. While this seems scandalous to us, it wasn't unheard of at the time.

When Hagar becomes pregnant, there is much rejoicing, but what happens next isn't too hard to predict. As Hagar's belly grows, so does her attitude. We can picture how awkward life must be in their home. Maybe Hagar drops things and asks Sarah to pick them up. Maybe she holds her aching back until Sarah feels obliged to clean the floor. Sarah must burn with irritation and anger, so she retaliates, making Hagar's life miserable.

Despondent, Hagar flees the home that had once been a haven to her and runs away into the desert. There, beside a spring, dejected and alone, she hears the voice of God speaking to her—not to one of God's chosen people but to her, a slave, a foreigner, a runaway. Out in the desert God sees one frightened slave girl who feels that no one sees her, and God speaks words that echo those spoken to His first runaway children in a garden: "Where are you?" (Genesis 3:9). No matter our status in other people's eyes, each one of us is worth a search and rescue operation to God.

God promises that her son will grow and thrive and be the leader of his own great nation. His name will be Ishmael, God says, "for the LORD has heard of your misery" (Genesis 16:11b). As God gives her son a name, Hagar gives a name to this God: the God who sees. God has seen Hagar and heard her misery.

Hagar is so moved that an insignificant and abandoned slave has significance in the eyes of Almighty God that she dries her eyes and willingly returns home where she gives birth to a son. She has fulfilled her end of the contract, but her problems have only begun.

There's not much mentioned about the boy Ishmael's formative years. There's no real indication that the relationship between Sarah and Hagar gets better. In fact, it seems to get worse when Sarah's own child finally arrives and Ishmael becomes competition for the new, favored child. As we learn in Genesis 21, fourteen years later, God miraculously provides the fulfillment of His promise with the long-awaited birth of baby Isaac. I imagine that as Sarah finally cradles her answered prayer in her arms, she can't seem to enjoy the moment. Ishmael and Hagar must be a constant reminder of her mistake and her lack of trust in God's plan.

Realizing that having two competing heirs in the same house will never have a good outcome, Sarah acts to protect her own son and schemes a second, terrible plan to erase the effects of her first. When she goes to Abraham, Sarah doesn't request this time. She orders, "Get rid of that slave woman and her son, for that woman's son will never share in the inheritance with my son Isaac" (Genesis 21:10).

Once again Hagar finds herself wandering into the desert, this time with her teenage son at her side. This time there's no home to return to, no family to welcome them back. It looks likely that they will both die in the desert. Once again God shows up. We learn that He is responding not to her weeping but to the boy's cries. This time, rather than guiding them safely home, God makes a home there in the desert for Hagar and her son. Instead of moving them out, God moves in.

Our experience is often similar, isn't it? Sometimes God rescues us from the desert, and sometimes God moves into the desert with us and makes it bloom. Easy circumstances are no proof of God's blessing, and difficult ones are no indication of His absence. Yet as we travel in and out of the desert seasons of our lives, we can know that God travels with us. We are never alone.

The Gift

With the arrival of their hoped-for Isaac, Abraham and Sarah's questions about God's reliability have been answered. But God has good reason to test *their* faithfulness. With their heart's desire in their arms, will they worship the Giver or begin worshiping the gift? So, God asks the unthinkable of Abraham: to sacrifice his

Abraham and Sarah

son. Even more surprising than God's command is Abraham's immediate and unquestioning response of obedience.

Abraham has been wandering and travelling since God first called him to leave his home, but this journey up Mount Moriah with Isaac in tow has to be the longest journey of his life. There is a lot of time to think. And there is Isaac right there behind him making his way along the path and following with a child's trustful gait.

Abraham builds an altar at the top. Then, taking Isaac is in his arms, he holds the gift close and offers him back to the Giver.

I have never had to face the decision Abraham faced. Neither have you. But at some point in our lives, all of us will hold someone we love in our arms and in our hearts, and we will be faced with a question: Will you entrust this person to God?

Nearly every time I get to the end of Abraham's story, I sigh in relief. God provides the sacrifice just as Abraham promised Isaac He would.

This God, the only True God, loves mercy not sacrifice. This is not a story about how God wants to take our children from us. He does not. God is the Giver. He is not to be confused with the one who comes to steal and kill and destroy (John 10:10). We don't need to fear this story, thinking that God will take away the things we love the most. In fact, it teaches us the opposite—that God can be trusted with our most precious gifts. They belong to Him first, after all. And God can be trusted with our lives.

When we are tempted to worry about our loved ones or our circumstances—to hold them too tightly or try to play god—we need to remember that the Giver of all good and perfect gifts loves them and us far more than we can imagine. And whatever the circumstance may be, God can take care of it!

God's plan is better than anything we can come up with on our own.

God is in control, so we don't have to be.

3

Isaac and Rebekah

Genesis 24-25

In Genesis 24, we find Isaac, the miracle baby born to Sarah and Abraham in their old age, all grown up but still a bachelor at age forty. This apparently concerns Isaac's aging father, Abraham, given his determination to find his son a wife. And the choice of a wife is no small decision. The woman Isaac will marry is destined to become the matriarch of a very important lineage, chosen by God to change the world.

The Search for a Wife

Not only does Isaac not get to choose a wife for himself; Abraham is too old to make the trip, so he sends his most trusted servant back to his homeland to find Isaac a wife from his own clan

Broken and Blessed

and tribe. The servant is never named, but since it is mentioned that this is Abraham's oldest and most trusted servant, many who study this passage assume that it is Eliezer.[3] Abraham once lamented that since he didn't have a son, his trusted servant Eliezer would become his heir (Genesis 15:2). That illustrates how close this relationship must be, blurring lines between friendship and family.

Clearly Abraham must have a high degree of confidence and a deep level of trust in his servant to ask him to choose a wife for his son. This man must know Abraham and his values well enough to choose as Abraham himself would choose.

From the beginning the servant understands that God's divine guidance will play a big part in the selection of Isaac's wife. And when he reaches his destination, prayer plays an important role in the fulfillment of his journey. Rather than praying for God to provide a wife for Isaac who is beautiful or brilliant or gifted or wealthy, he prays for a woman who is giving and selfless and has a heart to serve.

In his prayer, he describes a young woman who will not only do the favor he asks of her (serving him some water from the well) but also will volunteer to bring water for all of his camels,

Isaac and Rebekah

a task that some have calculated might involve hauling 250 gallons of water and taking several hours to complete.[4] The servant asks God to send Isaac a young woman who is in the habit of going above and beyond for others, who generously shares her time and resources with others.

That day Rebekah is simply going about her usual routine of serving her family by getting their daily water supply from the well. Having grown up in a culture that highly valued hospitality, Rebekah responds to the stranger's request for a drink of water because it is kind, welcoming, and the right thing to do. But then she goes far beyond what is asked, doing hours of extra work to provide for the needs of a stranger from a foreign land, someone who likely would never repay her kindness. She has no idea that her simple statement, "I will draw water for your camels, too," will lead to a husband, a fortune, a legacy, a place in history, and a place in eternity.

Once the servant has found Rebekah, his task is not quite fulfilled. He then has to convince her and gain her family's approval to accompany him back on an arduous journey to marry a man she has never met. The servant gives an elaborate speech, bragging on God's guidance

Broken and Blessed

and provision because he wants these relatives to understand, as he does, that God's hand is at work in their meeting. This might be an arranged marriage, he is saying, but it is truly God who is arranging it.

Rebekah's selfless attitude continues as her family consents to the proposal of marriage and agrees to send her back with the servant. It helps that they realize they are sending her to marry a close relative because her father is Abraham's nephew. What would be a liability today is actually a distinct benefit of this particular match.

Having completed his mission, the servant is anxious to get back home, but Rebekah's family wants her to stay another ten days or so. Possibly they want to throw a banquet in her honor as is the custom. Although their culture generally does not value the opinions of women, her parents ask Rebekah what she wants to do. Rebekah chooses to return with him, and her family blesses her.

We can learn an important lesson from Rebekah. Too often we focus on getting others to meet our expectations, rather than fulfilling God's expectations for our own behavior. It's always a good idea to work on being the kind

Isaac and Rebekah

of person we'd like others to be rather than working on changing others. Rather than trying to get others to measure up to our expectations, we should focus on our own behaviors. After all, there's only one person you can change, and that's yourself. All of our friendships and family relationships would probably improve if we followed Rebekah's example of showering others with kindness.

A Generation with Purpose

Isaac marries Rebekah, and Genesis 24:67 tells us that he loves her. In fact, this is the first time romantic love is mentioned in the Bible. Abraham's prayers have been answered, and the next generation is just around the corner.

Like the generations before and after them, Isaac and Rebekah struggle with infertility. Perhaps due to his awareness of the way God played a major role in his own parents' struggle to conceive a child, Isaac goes straight to God in prayer. Of the three generations, Isaac is the only one who simply prays first without trying to control or manipulate.

When Rebekah finally gets pregnant, it is a double blessing: twins! But she becomes concerned when the activity within her womb seems unusually violent, and she has no medical advice or ultrasound technology to take a peek. So Rebekah consults the only expert available to her, her Creator, to ask what is happening. God says to her:

> *"Two nations are in your womb,*
> *and two peoples from within you will be separated;*
> *one people will be stronger than the other,*
> *and the older will serve the younger."*
> Genesis 25:23

On the one hand, Rebekah learns that her fears are unfounded; the babies are fine. On the other hand, she discovers there are more serious worries ahead. The struggle is not only about fetuses battling for space or brothers who will spend most of their lives in conflict. The big picture involves a battle brewing between two nations.

How often do we, like Rebekah, base our concerns on our own limited experience and not

Isaac and Rebekah

God's perspective? Sometimes, like Rebekah, we need to stop and ask for God's perspective on our situation. Taking a God's-eye-view of things often helps us to see the larger purpose of the story we are living.

Even though Isaac and Rebekah are not leading characters in the Genesis family story, their story serves a purpose—and that purpose is not diminished by the faith that comes before them or the drama that comes after them. Isaac's name is listed among the great stories of his people, and this reminds us that we all have a place in history.

You, too, have a purpose to fulfill in your generation. Your name may not end up in history books, but you have a unique calling in your generation; and God is cheering you on as you fulfill it.

God has given each of us a purpose to fulfill.

It begins with being the kind of person we'd like others to be.

4

Jacob and Esau

Genesis 25, 27, 33

Jacob and Esau present the most colorful biblical account of a sibling pair. From their earliest days, beginning in utero, the life of these twins is filled with conflict and strife. They are born into an imperfect family whose practices of favoritism poison their relationship and lead to full-blown sibling rivalry. We can learn much from their story.

Sibling Rivalry

As twins, we might expect Jacob and Esau to be similar, but they are different in every way. From the beginning, Jacob is portrayed as a grasping, conniving character. At birth, his

Jacob and Esau

chubby, little newborn hand firmly clutches his older brother's heel, as though Jacob is saying, "Oh, no, you don't!" as he tries to stop his twin from being born first. Based on their first view of him, his parents name him Grabby, which in Hebrew translates as Jacob. The name is fitting in more ways than one, since it also refers to a person who deceives or supplants, one who tries to take what is not his.

The origin of their names foretells just how different the brothers will be. Jacob's name is symbolic, action-driven, laced with a subversive, hidden meaning. Esau, on the other hand, is named at face value. His name comes from a simple, knee-jerk reaction to his appearance. Quite the unusual baby, Esau is born covered in hair, so his parents name him Hairy (Esau in Hebrew). He is ruddy and red, so his nickname is Edom (Red).

Esau grows up to be a face-value kind of guy. With him, you always know what you are getting. He is hairy, outdoorsy, and loves to hunt. When he sees something he wants, he simply takes it without the underhanded deception of Jacob.

How can two people who come from the same mix of DNA, share the same womb, and grow up

Broken and Blessed

in the same household be so different? That's a question that parents have been asking about their children since the beginning of time.

As the story of Jacob and Esau develops, we may be tempted to demonize Jacob and feel sorry for Esau as the mistreated and misunderstood brother. But we must remember that no family story is that simple. When you find a family that has a single "problem child" (or adult) who causes trouble for everyone else, it's almost certain that this individual is not the only problem. Families operate as very interdependent systems, and one problem rising to the surface usually means there are additional troubles in the mix.

Esau isn't just an innocent victim as he's often made out to be. He is impulsive and short-sighted. He doesn't value the inheritance that awaits him or his position of authority in the family. In fact, Scripture tells us that he despises his birthright (Genesis 25:34).

Jacob doesn't have the rank or strength of his older and stronger brother, Esau, so he turns to wit, cunning, and political savvy. But it's the way that he uses them for his own gain, without consideration for his brother, that taints his reputation.

Jacob and Esau

Jacob and Esau, however, are not solely to blame in the family fight that ensues. Their parents actually set the stage for the ongoing competition and conflict that characterizes their sons' lives. Genesis 25:28 tells us that Isaac favors Esau and Rachel loves Jacob.

Combine the favoritism of both parents, the inequity of the way their culture favors the oldest boy in the family, and the ambition of the youngest in this family, and you have a powder-keg of relationships ready to explode.

Birthright and Blessing

Jacob and Esau are born in a time when the one who happens to be born first will receive both the family birthright and the blessing. The birthright is a disproportionately large share of the inheritance and the right to take his father's place as family patriarch. His position as firstborn would, upon the death of his father, make him ruler of the family, including his siblings. The blessing is the confirmation that the oldest is the heir and new head of the family as well as the spiritual inheritance of God's favor and blessing.

Both the birthright and blessing belonged exclusively to the oldest simply because he is first, even if only by a few seconds. That injustice troubles Jacob from childhood. What is so special about Esau that he should inherit the entire estate? Jacob fumes and plots and waits.

His opportunity finally comes when Esau returns from a hunting trip empty-handed and exhausted, declaring, "I'm starving to death; what's there to eat around here?" It just happens that Jacob, little Grabby, has been cooking something up in more ways than one.

Jacob is eating the last bowl of food in the house, a red stew. Even if there are more ingredients to prepare another batch, this is not the era of "fast food." Esau wants food to eat *now*. Jacob knows that Esau is hungry and vulnerable. He also knows what he wants for himself, and he goes after it. Jacob has been "stewing" to get what belongs to Esau since their birth. So he introduces the deal that will change both of their lives: Esau's birthright for one bowl of stew. Esau agrees and the deal is sealed.

Note that it's not only Jacob who is at fault here, living up to his name's meaning: "Grabby"

Jacob and Esau

or "Deceiver." Esau has let himself run on empty so long that he is willing to take part in a bargain that will fill his stomach but empty his future.

This episode ends with both brothers having what they want but neither of them being truly satisfied. Esau's bowl of food will satisfy for only a time, and he will be hungry again, this time without an inheritance in his pocket. Jacob's newly acquired birthright is the beginning of an underhanded series of events that will cause so much turmoil in the family that he will have to run away, making it impossible for him to enjoy the land, inheritance, and leadership he has seized. The lesson for all of us is that grabbing for the things that look so good on someone else's plate never brings us happiness in the end.

Jacob has shown that he will do anything to get ahead of his brother, Esau. But he will not rest until he has taken everything, including his brother's blessing as well. This blessing is a serious commodity passed from a father on his deathbed to his eldest son, with serious spiritual and material significance. This moment of blessing is like the signing of a will, where the father states his personal wishes that this oldest son will inherit and rule the estate. The spiritual significance of the blessing means that God's special relationship with this family is handed down through the generations.

In Genesis 27, we find Jacob stooping to his lowest point. When he swiped Esau's birthright, he at least met his brother face-to-face and got his consent, no matter how underhanded his dealings were. In the story of the blessing, however, Jacob deceives his own dying father by dressing up as his brother. He lies multiple times, claiming to be Esau. He even invokes the name of God in Genesis 27:20. Jacob strengthens his story of deception by saying that God has given him success.

Yet despite all of his scheming, Jacob does not act alone. Rebekah, Jacob's mother, is the one who overhears the conversation when Isaac asks Esau to go hunting for game and prepare his favorite dish. She is the one who conceives the plan and convinces Jacob. And she is the one who literally dresses him, covering him in his brother's clothes and the hide of an animal to give him the feel of his hairy brother, Esau.

By choosing to bless one child instead of both, Isaac and Rebekah bring curses on the family

Jacob and Esau

relationships. Isaac's favoritism of Esau sours his wife and younger son toward him to the point that they are willing to deceive him on his deathbed. Rebekah's manipulation to win success for her favorite son means that she will lose the trust of one son and the company of the other when he has to flee because of his mother's schemes.

Though giving a "blessing" may seem to us like a mostly ceremonial and empty act, in this culture and specifically for this family, the blessing is a very serious and valuable commodity. We know this because Rebekah willingly manipulates her entire family and risks the relationships she values most so that her favorite son will receive the blessing. Isaac trembles violently when he realizes that he has given his blessing to the wrong son. And poor Esau cries out in despair, begging his father to bless him too (Genesis 27:34).

There is a lesson for us at this point in the story. Unlike the heartbreak we witness Esau experiencing, we never have to wonder if there is enough blessing to go around. Unlike Jacob, we don't have to trick our Father into blessing us. He is always eager to give blessings to His children. Central to the call from God that Abraham and

Sarah received was the message that they and their family were blessed to be a blessing (Genesis 12:1-2). God's blessings are free-flowing and abundant; they are meant to be shared.

A Surprise Ending

We find ourselves now at a dramatic highpoint in the story. Because of Esau's hatred and rage, Jacob has to flee. Jacob and Esau weren't that many generations removed from the very first brothers, Cain and Abel, and that story of sibling rivalry didn't have such a great ending. In fact, I believe that Cain and Abel are the reason that parents spend so much energy trying to prevent that scenario from happening all over again! Remembering that story and knowing how enraged Esau would be, Jacob's mother sent her Jacob off to stay with her brother and his family in a distant country. He was gone for decades, separated from his family. Though the land was now legally his, he couldn't even inhabit it for fear of the brother from whom he had stolen it. Sibling rivalry had separated him from the inheritance he had stolen as well as the family who loved him.

Years later, when Jacob decides to return home, he is understandably hesitant. There is no way of knowing the extent of Esau's anger or how he might take revenge. During his journey home, Jacob learns that Esau is coming to meet him accompanied by four hundred men. This sounds more like a war party than a welcoming party. Now, for the first time, instead of grasping other people's gifts, Jacob becomes a giver and sends gifts ahead to Esau as a peace offering.

The beautiful surprise ending is that Esau accepts Jacob's gifts and forgives his brother. In Genesis 33:10, Jacob compares seeing Esau's face to seeing the face of God—a fact that acknowledges Esau's forgiveness and indicates the heart change within Jacob. Their story is resolved with reconciliation, offering hope for the conflicts within our own families.

Two Prodigals

There's a beautiful parable that Jesus told about a father and two sons and a family drama over inheritance. Those who listened to Jesus tell this story would have immediately recognized some

Broken and Blessed

similarities with Jacob and Esau's story. Both focus on family betrayal and the resulting conflict between two sons. In both Jacob's true life story and the story Jesus told about the prodigal, the younger sons receive their inheritance through dishonorable means, run away and seek happiness elsewhere, forfeit their inheritance (Jacob because he is not home to enjoy what is now his, and the prodigal because it has all been spent), care for livestock while they are away from home (Jacob cares for his uncle Laban's goats while the prodigal cares for pigs), and reach a breaking point and return home.

Despite their apprehension in returning home, both younger sons are welcomed with open arms. Although Jacob approaches with gifts and the prodigal has none, in both stories we see that welcome is not based on worthiness. In fact, one of the most beautiful parallels between the two stories is the reception the two young men receive from their relative. Genesis 33:4 and Luke 15:20 are the only two places in Scripture where we find this exact description of running toward someone, throwing arms around him, and kissing him. The similarity between the stories becomes undeniably strong at this point. Those listening to Jesus' story would have noticed a very clear connection and leaned in closer to hear how Jesus would resolve the story. Clearly the father in the prodigal story is meant to mirror our heavenly Father, who eagerly awaits our return when we stray from Him and accepts us just as we are.

Both stories show us that God reveals Himself in the faces of those who offer forgiveness. When we are called to forgive others, our actions can reflect God's face and God's love. Yet unlike Jacob's story, in which we see an attitude of scarcity—an attitude that there is not enough to go around for all—Jesus' parable reveals God's attitude toward us, which is one of abundance and blessing. May we never forget that God always has more than enough blessings for all His children—enough to satisfy all our needs.

Forgiveness reflects God's love.

God has enough blessings for all our needs.

5

Rachel and Leah

Genesis 29-30

After reading the story of Jacob and Esau, you may think that no sibling story can match the struggles of this pair of brothers. But I'd like to introduce you to a set of sisters—also in this same generation of the Genesis family—that rival their status of "worst siblings ever."

Blinded by Love

The story of these two sisters begins in the middle of Jacob and Esau's story. After swindling his brother's birthright and stealing his blessing, Jacob leaves town and sets off for a distant country to stay with relatives. Jacob arrives at his destination and finds himself at a well. The second meeting of a wife by a well in this family might seem especially coincidental (or providential) to us, but in those days a village well was a popular

Rachel and Leah

public gathering place, especially for women who performed many of the household duties.

Jacob has just asked some local shepherds about his mother's brother, Laban, when an attractive shepherdess and her flock approach. As if on cue, the shepherds quip: "As a matter of fact, here comes Laban's daughter now!" Whether or not Jacob remembers stories of his grandfather's servant selecting his mother at a well in the same area, he is instantly taken with Rachel. He finds out the shepherds are waiting for all the flocks to gather and for someone to roll the stone away from the front of the well so they can all water their sheep. When Rachel approaches, Jacob flexes his muscles and shows off his strength by rolling the stone in front of the well away. Then he waters his uncle's sheep as an act of service.

Jacob then weeps for joy with honest emotion and kisses Rachel as he shares the news that he is a close relative visiting from a far off land. Just as the servant who brokered the marriage deal between Jacob's parents—Isaac and Rebekah—was taken directly from the well to meet Rebekah's brother, Laban, so Rachel immediately takes Jacob to meet her father, who just so happens to be Laban.

Broken and Blessed

Jacob was given explicit instructions from his father to marry one of Laban's daughters, so I'm sure he counted himself lucky when he discovered that's exactly who this beautiful young woman was. What he didn't know yet was that Laban had two daughters, and that simple fact set off enough drama to fill his life for many years.

Genesis 29:16-17 tells us about the two sisters. Rachel is described as having a lovely figure and as beautiful. And the only description we hear about Leah involves her eyes. The Hebrew word used to describe Leah's eyes, *rakkot*, is often translated "weak," possibly referring to her eyesight or a medical problem with her eyes.[5] The best-case scenario (for Leah anyway) is that it may be a compliment, since the phrase also can be translated "delicate eyes." The passage raves about Rachel, but when it comes to Leah, all it says is she has nice eyes. This might be the equivalent of us saying that one sister was gorgeous and the other had a "nice personality." Can't you see the strain of comparison between these two sisters?

The problems for Jacob begin when he and Laban strike a deal. Jacob will work for Laban for seven years as payment for marrying the daughter who is lovely. There is no handshake

Rachel and Leah

on this deal, no covenant made, no celebratory meal described. Jacob takes Laban at his word, a mistake he will regret. Even the crafty Jacob can be blinded by love, and he lets his guard down.

Laban tells Jacob that they are kin. Their similarities are lost on Jacob at first, but later he may recognize the family traits of manipulation that have been passed from Eve to Sarah to his mother, Rebekah, and her brother, Laban.

Here Comes the Bride(s)

Although Jacob's understanding is that he is toiling for seven years to win the hand of Rachel, who is beautiful, Laban has other plans. So when the seven years are complete and the wedding arrives, Laban sets his plan into motion and throws a feast in honor of his daughter's wedding. But rather than giving Jacob his younger daughter, Rachel, he secretly gives his older daughter, Leah, instead.

Jacob, possibly having feasted a little more than his limit, stumbles into a dark tent with a veiled bride and doesn't realize until the morning that he has been duped. He thinks he is going to bed with the beautiful Rachel but awakes with the less desirable Leah.

Broken and Blessed

The plot of this story unfolds masterfully with suspense and humor. As the onlookers, we know that Jacob has been tricked, and we are waiting for the other shoe to drop and the realization to hit him. His confrontation of Laban is a strangely satisfying episode because we recognize that Jacob has been wronged and, at the same time, is getting what he has coming.

In perfect symmetry Jacob, the younger brother who has swindled his older brother out of his entitlements, becomes the victim of a plot where the older daughter seizes what was supposed to belong to the younger. Jacob sees his own flaws reflected in his Uncle Laban, and he's experiencing firsthand the kind of pain and disappointment that he caused to his own brother. And just as Jacob offered no apology to Esau, Laban offers no apology to Jacob. Instead he offers another deal.

If this kind of deceptive switcheroo happened today, the situation probably would produce a quick annulment or divorce. In their culture, the answer was marrying the second sister as well, since polygamy was a common practice.

We don't know when Rachel and Leah are brought up to speed on their father's plot to

Rachel and Leah

deceive their future husband, but they at least have to go along with it by the wedding night. As we watch the story unfold, remember that Rachel and Leah are living in a time when women are relegated to background roles in a rather mundane existence. Their wedding feast is one of the few times they are given honor and attention. Both women probably have been looking forward to their weddings since they were little girls, knowing that the elaborate celebration will last up to two weeks with all of their family and friends in attendance and them at the center.

Just think how Rachel must feel when, after the first week of her wedding feast, her father chooses to give her husband to her sister instead. And consider how Leah must feel being robbed of her own moment in the spotlight. She even has to endure the look of horror on her husband's face at the realization that he has married her. Even though a deal is struck that means they will finish the second half of the feast for what is Leah's wedding celebration and continue immediately into Rachel's wedding celebration, those must be parties that are more bitter than sweet for both young women. These two sisters are being set up for a life together under the same roof married to the same man—one in which they will continue to compete for attention, affection, and love.

Let me pause to acknowledge that, like Rachel and Leah, some of us have been wronged deeply by those we trust. Like Jacob, at times our heartfelt hopes and expectations have not been met. And yet in another scene of deception within this imperfect family, we see that God continues to walk beside them. God is not surprised, nor are His plans foiled, by Laban's tricks. He continues to sing over Rachel in her disappointment and to see beauty in Leah when she feels ignored. And in your own story, God continues to watch over you, too, no matter where you find yourself.

A Competition No One Can Win

Rachel and Leah began their marriages to the same man within a week of each other. If anyone ever felt the sting of competition, these two sisters found themselves embroiled in a family drama that is hard for us to even imagine. Arranged marriage and polygamy are foreign concepts to us, but the idea that two sisters could be married to the same man at the same time is unthinkable. Anyone could guess that this arrangement is a disaster waiting to happen.

None of the relationships within this familial love triangle are prepped for success, especially because both sisters find themselves in a situation where they do not have the thing they long for most.

Leah is the underdog in the beginning because of her looks and the way her father deceived her husband into marrying her. It's very clear that Jacob is in love with Rachel but has to take Leah as part of the package.

Rachel may be the best-loved by their husband, but she's unable to have children, a fact that causes her great pain and distress. (Note that this is the third generation in this family that struggles with infertility—a theme I explore in the *Broken and Blessed* Bible study.)

Leah has several sons right away, and Rachel is worried that her sister is pulling ahead in this competition. So Rachel comes

Broken and Blessed

up with the ingenious plan to give her servant, Bilhah, to Jacob to bear children. Sound familiar? This is the same plan that caused Sarah so much trouble with Hagar and Ishmael. I wonder if Rachel realizes that this plan has already been used by Jacob's grandmother, and it didn't work out so well.

Leah, not to be outdone, pulls the same trick by having her maid Zilpah bear children with Jacob. Now we have four women in the same household sleeping with the same man.

Unfortunately for the children who are born, Rachel and Leah use them to keep score in their rivalry. They're not the first family, nor are they the last, to use their children to compete, compare, and try to win status. As you well know, this kind of ranking-by-children still goes on today. In the end, Rachel bears Jacob two sons. Her story has a sad ending, though, because she dies giving birth to her younger son.

I wonder how Leah mourned her sister's death. Did she grieve the years they lost by being in constant competition? Did she grieve the relationship they might have had, the support they might have given, the gift

Rachel and Leah

of watching each other's children grow up in the same house with love and support and affection? And then Leah was left alone to care for the whole brood, her children as well as her sister's. When family members compete, no one wins in the end.

Rachel and Leah remind us that God created families to operate as teams, not as competitors. When one family member hurts, we all hurt. When one family member succeeds, we all win. Instead of competing for some invisible rank in life, we do better to see our family members as teammates—supporting and encouraging them with our words, our presence, and our affirmation.

Comparison leads to pride or discontent; competition destroys relationships.

Our family members are our teammates, not our rivals.

6

Joseph and His Brothers

Genesis 37, 39-50

We've come now to the last major generation of the Genesis family and the dramatic story of Jacob's twelve sons. In the tradition of Cain and Abel, Isaac and Ishmael, and Jacob and Esau, we have a battle of the brothers brewing as Joseph is favored over his older brothers. If pitting one brother against another caused turmoil in previous generations, showing preference to one brother while multiple older brothers watch causes mayhem even beyond this family's standards.

A Favored Son

An obvious demonstration of Jacob's favoritism is when he gives Joseph an expensive robe of many colors. The garment is not just a token of

Joseph and His Brothers

love for the father's favorite; it is a symbol of leadership and succession. Jacob gives Joseph a robe to mark him as heir. In a culture where birth order determines everyone's role and position in a family, this is a shocking declaration. By choosing Joseph as his heir, Jacob is circumventing the cultural rules about the firstborn (which he obviously never adhered to anyway) and naming the first son of his favorite wife as the next in line to rule the family.

Joseph's attitude doesn't help his cause. He may be the eventual hero of this story, but in the beginning he's described at age seventeen as a tattletale (Genesis 37:2), a braggart, and a brat. To make matters worse, he tells his brothers about two dreams he has in which he is ruling over them. In presenting the dreams, Joseph is either naïve, unwittingly stirring up his brothers' anger, or intentionally confrontational, rubbing salt in the already raw family wounds.

Between their father's preferential treatment and Joseph's dreaming and bragging, the brothers have plenty of reasons to develop a deep hatred for Joseph. It's no wonder that not too far into their story they begin plotting to kill him.

Broken and Blessed

From Favored Son to Slave to Second-hand Man

In the midst of the brothers' murderous schemes, two of the brothers come to Joseph's defense. Reuben encourages the brothers not to kill him but to throw him in a pit and leave him. Another brother, Judah, sees a band of traders passing by as an opportunity to suggest that they sell Joseph into slavery. Though harsh treatment, this may be what prevents Joseph's death.

After killing a goat and covering Joseph's coat with blood, the brothers return home with the bloodstained coat, letting Jacob draw his own conclusions. He pledges to mourn for his favorite son until his own death.

Formerly a favored son, Joseph finds himself a slave, yet somehow he makes the best of it. He prospers as the second in command to his master Potiphar, and the leadership gifts that came across as pride in his youth now develop into full flower.

Then tragedy comes again to Joseph; his master's wife has him thrown in prison when he refuses to sleep with her. While in prison, Joseph befriends two other wrongfully imprisoned servants and interprets their cryptic dreams, one for better and one for worse. Once again he's not afraid to be honest when the dream of one man means that he will be put to death. The other servant returns to Pharaoh's household and forgets about Joseph's service to him until Pharaoh himself experiences a vivid and disturbing dream. Suddenly, the memory of Joseph's gifts is stirred, and Joseph is brought to Pharaoh to see if he can decipher the meaning of Pharaoh's dream.

Pharaoh's dream means that tough times are ahead for Egypt. Instead of simply dropping the news of a severe famine in Pharaoh's lap, Joseph also proposes a set of sensible solutions, suggesting that "Pharaoh look for a discerning and wise man and put him in charge of the land of Egypt" to prepare the country for the worst (Genesis 41:33). Pharaoh recognizes the gifts of discernment and leadership in Joseph and elevates him to be his right-hand man.

Revenge or Reconciliation?

As it turns out, Pharaoh's dream comes true. After seven years of abundance, seven years of

Broken and Blessed

famine hit Egypt and the international community hard. Joseph's role as second in command in the kingdom becomes a matter of life and death as Pharaoh tells all the Egyptians: "Go to Joseph and do what he tells you" (Genesis 41:55).

Joseph has the country prepared for this difficult time. Not only are Egypt's storehouses well stocked; they begin to provide international aid to other countries affected. In the middle of all the refugees heading to Egypt for grain is a group of ten brothers who have traveled far to get food to save their family. They do not recognize the powerful man before whom they are forced to beg for grain. Joseph is older, probably clean-shaven and clothed in the dress of Egyptian rulers. But he recognizes his brothers immediately. It seems he is wrestling with how to handle this reunion, since the decision between revenge and reconciliation lies completely in his hands.

While the brothers see only one side of the story, we see a man who is struggling with confronting his past and what to do with the power he now wields over the brothers who wronged him. For three chapters (42-44) he toys with them like a cat with vulnerable prey, first keeping one brother in prison while sending the rest of them home to

Joseph and His Brothers

guarantee he will see them again. Then he sends them home with bags stuffed with grain and the insistence that they return with their younger brother Benjamin. On the way home they realize that the money they paid for the grain is still in their bags. Joseph repaid the grain fee secretly, but to the brothers it seems they accidentally shoplifted from a very powerful man.

When later they must return for more grain, they know that they must bring Benjamin as part of the deal. The terrible burden this separation brings to their father reveals how protective the whole family is of Benjamin.

The calloused exterior Joseph shows to the brothers is almost exposed when Joseph lays eyes on Benjamin for the first time. Seeing "his own mother's son" (43:29), for whom he clearly has a fondness, almost puts Joseph over the edge.

In Chapter 44, the tender Joseph gives way once again to the angry tyrant. Joseph falsely accuses Benjamin of stealing and insists that he will make Benjamin his slave and force the brothers to return home without him, an act that might kill their father with grief. The once heartless brothers are beside themselves with concern for Benjamin and for their father. Suddenly, Judah shocks them all by proposing a revolutionary solution: he will sacrifice his life so that Benjamin will have a future and their father will be spared immense grief. This single act melts Joseph's heart and allows healing to begin in the family.

It is significant that Judah's act of sacrifice changes the course for this family. Many years later, God's own Son, Jesus, will be born into the tribe of Judah; and His sacrifice will bring the greatest blessing the world has ever known. The lineage of sacrifice that turns the tide for Joseph's family will bring the ultimate sacrifice that will bring blessing to all people.

The moment Joseph hears Judah pledge to serve as a slave in exchange for Benjamin's freedom, Joseph sends all the Egyptians out of the room, comes down from his place of authority to approach his brothers, and reveals his identity. They are afraid for their lives, but Joseph reassures them that his attitude toward them is one of forgiveness.

Joseph finds the courage to pursue a path of peace for the future of this family. For generations this family has lived with a script of competition and revenge. Though Jacob and his brother, Esau, had an encounter of forgiveness, we have no record of their relationship after that moment to know if the relationship was fully restored. Yet unlike his ancestors, Joseph chooses to forgive his brothers and live in peace with them. He is the family member who breaks the family cycle and begins a new way of relating within the family.

Blessed to Be a Blessing

As we come to the end of the Genesis story, we find this family living together in Egypt in a pocket of peace and prosperity despite the famine going on around them. Jacob knows that he is in his last days. When the time comes for him to give a blessing to his son and heir, instead of summoning just one favorite son he calls all of his boys around him. The tender scene in Genesis 49 is one of family togetherness made possible only because of God's overwhelming blessing that already has changed the course of their family.

Jacob gives a blessing to every one of his sons. Granted, some of the sons have a checkered past and a questionable future, and so some of the blessings are more challenging than others. But Jacob places his hand on each of his twelve sons, speaks words about their future, and acknowledges that they are special individuals.

Jacob not only blesses all of his sons, but later he also adopts Joseph's sons, Ephraim and Manasseh, as his very own. These boys, who might have been considered second-class citizens with their Egyptian birth and upbringing, are lifted up as sons who are central to the bright future of their family in the land God has given them.

What powerful lessons we find in this story! Joseph chooses forgiveness and reconciliation rather than revenge, and he changes the course of history for his family. We too can be change agents in our families. God is calling each of us to be a new creation, to chart a new course as the first generation that chooses a new path.

Joseph also is able to see God's hand at work even in the toughest of situations, telling his brothers, "You intended to harm me, but God intended it for good to accomplish what is now being done, the saving of many lives" (Genesis 50:20). This should encourage us! Whatever struggles we may see, God's blessings are always at work behind the scenes, taking what was meant for harm and bringing God's goodness in the end.

We also see in this story a picture of God's abundant blessings and lavish love, flowing from Israel to his sons and from there to the twelve tribes that they will become. We see that God has

Joseph and His Brothers

more than enough blessing to go around. He is always abundantly bringing goodness and mercy to us so that those blessings may overflow.

Finally, God not only blesses us; He adopts us into His family! Just as Jacob adopted Ephraim and Manasseh as his very own sons, we too are welcomed into the family of God because of what He has done through His son, Jesus. The perfect Son of God was born into this imperfect, broken family—and He gave his life so that we might be adopted into the family. Jesus came so that we could receive forgiveness, reconciliation, blessing, and adoption—and then share these gifts with others. As followers of Jesus, we are members of the family of God—God's secret weapon. Our job is to pass on God's love in a hurting, broken world. And it all begins in that perfectly imperfect place we call family.

God is calling us, His children, to be change agents in our families and our world.

Despite our brokenness, we are blessed to be a blessing.

Notes

1. "Adamah," http://biblesuite.com/hebrew/127.htm.
2. "Adam," http://biblesuite.com/hebrew/120.htm.
3. Gerhard von Rand, *Genesis: A Commentary* (Philadelphia: Westminster Press, 1972), p. 254.
4. Keith Krell, "The Fingerprints of God," https://bible.org/seriespage/fingerprints-god-genesis-241-67.
5. Leon Kass, *The Beginning of Wisdom* (Chicago: University of Chicago Press, 2003), p. 423.